$21.95

NEW ORLEANS JAZZ FEST

Lewis Johnson, Norris Lewis, and Sherman Washington with the Zion Harmonizers, 1982   2078/19

NEW ORLEANS JAZZ FEST

A Pictorial History

MICHAEL P. SMITH

Foreword by
BEN SANDMEL

PELICAN PUBLISHING COMPANY
Gretna 1991

Library of Congress Cataloging-in-Publication Data

Smith, Michael P. (Michael Proctor), 1937–
    New Orleans Jazz Fest : a pictorial history / by Michael P. Smith
; foreword by Ben Sandmel.
        p.   cm.
    Includes index.
    ISBN 0-88289-810-8
    1. New Orleans Jazz & Heritage Festival — Pictorial works.   2. Jazz
festivals — Louisiana — New Orleans — Pictorial works.   I. Title.
ML38.N28N447   1991
781.65′079′76335 — dc20   90-25055
                                                                           CIP
                                                                           MN

The New Orleans Jazz & Heritage Festival is staged annually by the
New Orleans Jazz & Heritage Foundation, Inc., a nonprofit corpora-
tion dedicated to this purpose and to preserving and fostering the
rich music and cultural heritage of New Orleans and Louisiana. The
publisher acknowledges that the marks "Jazz Fest" and "New Orleans
Jazz Festival" are registered marks of the New Orleans Jazz & Heritage Foundation, Inc.

Manufactured in the United States of America
Published by Pelican Publishing Company, Inc.
1101 Monroe Street, Gretna, Louisiana 70053

This work is dedicated to the New Orleans Jazz & Heritage Festival staff...all the people who do the many months of preproduction, production, and postproduction, most of whose names and contributions can be found in each year's Official Souvenir Program Book. Few people appreciate how much time and work and how many people are involved in the production of each year's festival. More than 250 individuals were named as key personnel last year alone. The principals of this staff are George Wein, Quint Davis, Bob Jones, Allison Miner, Vicky Bell, Charlie Bering, Nancy Ochsenschlager, Karlton Kirksey, Tague Richardson, John ("Klondike") Koehler, John Murphy, Parker Dinkins, Henry Hildebrand III, Kelly Sullivan, Anna Zimmerman, Susan Mock, Louis Edwards, Camille Hardy, Sally Gates Cobb, Khalid Hafiz, Dawn Griffin, Linda Berry, Dodie Smith-Simmons, Laura Laughlin, Stephanie Samuel, Dee Lindsey, Sherman Washington, Reverend Ott, Ifama Arsan, Sandra Blair-Richardson, Vera Warren, Norman Dixon, Rhonda Ford, Mike Noble, Lloyd and Laura Cottingim, Garnet Hardin, Eddie Lambert, Phillip ("Wiredog") Cobb, Frank Hayward, Rocky Ruiz, John Kelly, Tim Bernett, George Porter, Ed White, Chuck Blamphin, Howie Hodes, Raymond ("Choo Choo") Belamy, Juan Labroste, William Brower, and Smokey Dugas. These people and their assistants take care of everything from building the sites, Heritage Fair and evening concert production, to ground transportation, security, sanitation, and medical services. Thank you.

Sharkey Bonano & the Kings of Jazz: Monk Hazel (drums), Chink Martin (bass), Harry Shields (saxophone), 1970   365/17a

Contents

Duke Ellington, Mahalia Jackson, George Wein, and Cousin Joe, 1970   359/30a

Foreword

In 1970, the first New Orleans Jazz & Heritage Festival drew a crowd of several hundred people to a small site in Congo Square. Today, festival attendance is pushing a quarter of a million, on a site of thirty-five acres. Despite this transformation, the Jazz Fest's core concepts remain unchanged: to celebrate Louisiana's unique cultural riches, in terms of music, cuisine, and crafts; to proudly present them to the world, with emphasis on the African/Caribbean/French continuum; to enhance and encourage their growth and preservation.

In recent years this vision has been logically extended to include a variety of global genres, presenting New Orleans as a musical and cultural crossroads. Such creative ideas are implemented through equally innovative programming, and if it all sounds rather serious, the results couldn't be more down-to-earth and fun. Jazz Fest time is now a full-fledged seasonal ritual in New Orleans, on a par with Mardi Gras or the Christmas holidays.

The Jazz Fest has also entered its third decade — reached legal age, if you will — and the attainment of this milestone calls for celebration, reminiscence, and a bit of introspection. Michael Smith's photos and observations and the memoirs of various festival participants merge here to look inside a small, local event, its transformation into a world-class expression of regional culture, and its emergence as a major venue for global talent in the Deep South.

A text of this length cannot provide a comprehensive, definitive history of the Jazz Fest, and no claim is made to do so. Just as it was difficult to limit the selection of photos here, there were equally hard choices to be made amidst a wealth of excellent interviews. What follows, rather, is an assemblage of oral history, personal narrative, opinions, and insights, all focussing on the New Orleans institution that is the Jazz Fest. Many other people have equally worthy stories to tell, and perhaps another forum will include their perspectives, too.

"The current New Orleans Jazz & Heritage Festival was George Wein's concept and vision," Quint Davis begins. "There was another organization, headed up by Durel Black, that put on several festivals in the late sixties, prior to ours. They asked George to produce a concert series here, and he insisted instead on a traditional-music, multi-area ethnic event — like Pete Seeger had initiated at the Newport Folk Festival. George's thinking was that anyone could put on concerts, and that doing so wouldn't begin to tap all of New Orleans' resources. The first daytime, multistage festival at Congo Square in 1970 — which we named Louisiana Heritage Fair — was the genesis of both today's Jazz Fest, and today's New Orleans Jazz & Heritage Foundation.

"At that first festival," Davis continues, "Mahalia Jackson had done a night concert, and she came out to the fair one afternoon, at Congo Square, just to check it out. And she got fired up, and spontaneously started singing 'Just a Closer Walk with Thee,' with Percy Humphrey and the Eureka Brass Band [see next chapter]. That performance defined the whole tone of everything that the New Orleans Jazz & Heritage Festival could ever do and be — a New Orleans Gospel singer making a bridge between Gospel music and traditional New Orleans jazz, singing a hymn with a marching brass band. To me, that was the eternal spark of what the whole festival was forever going to be about.

"Allison Miner and I were both working for Dick Allen at the Tulane Jazz Archives," Davis says, explaining the origins of the festival's staff. "Dick told George Wein, 'I got these kids here who hang out and listen to music.' Allison and I met with George at Cafe du Monde, and he hired us to book the local bands."

"Quint and I went to clubs, bars, and churches," Miner remembers, "meeting people and telling them about the festival. It was all very loose, those first two years; neither of us had a car or a phone, and we did it all by riding busses and using the pay-phones at Allgood's Restaurant. In '72, when we moved to the current site [the infield of the Fair Grounds Race Track], we had invaluable help from three people in particular. Parker Dinkins coordinated all the legal details with the city, among many other duties. John Murphy wrote all the promotional and press material, and became the first fair director. And Henry Hildebrand initiated the crafts fair. They all deserve a lot of credit.

"I yearn for those old days, in some ways," Miner goes on. "What was most fun was when performers stayed at our houses, before we had a budget for hotels. People like Big Joe Williams, Bukka White, the Como Drum and Fife Corps. We would all eat meals together, and get to know each other. I can remember Robert Pete Williams, the great Louisiana blues guitarist, sitting in my living room regaling us for hours with fabulous ghost stories. That kind of thing doesn't happen anymore. When I initiated the Heritage Tent stage in 1988, it was to bring back an environment where people could communicate with the musicians on a conversational level, and feel as if they had touched them."

"Big Joe Williams decided that he was going to show us how to cook catfish," Quint Davis recollects ruefully. "He said he was the world's best catfish cook. And he covered four walls and the floor and hallway with grease — it was like a grease explosion. The apartment was never the same again. I'll bet the walls still drip up there."

The idealism of that era was also important to the Jazz Fest's building crew. Tague Richardson, who started as a carpenter in 1974, and is now the Heritage Fair's site director, remembers that conditions during his first year were strictly primitive. This was the third year of operations at the Fair Grounds, and the entire site budget was only $900. In lieu of scaffolding the crew would stand on the roof of old pickup trucks. "But money wasn't important," Richardson recalls, "because there was such a great feeling of camaraderie and brotherhood. We all loved the music, loved the festival, and gave it all we had. After work we'd have huge jam sessions. Everyone would play some instrument, even if they were just beating on garbage cans. There was a very close-knit family feeling. It's still there, but now business and money get in the way, and that tends to stifle the creative juices.

"I absolutely didn't think," Richardson reflects, "that the Jazz Fest would ever grow so big, and become a mega event. I've always felt privileged to be part of it, and I hope that I always will be. But I've always realized, watching its flow and growth, that no one person is essential to its perpetuation. The concept — the festival itself — is its own entity, and if one of us dies there can still be a festival."

One manifestation of the festival's emergence as an entity has been the growing influence of its board of directors. When enough income became available to give this board a working budget, a variety of programs was introduced to expand the festival's scope and embrace the local community. High priority is given to the hiring of black staff members. Tom Dent, the Jazz & Heritage Foundation's executive director, explains this stance, which is often perceived as anti-white. "We wouldn't feel right about pushing the issue if the Jazz Fest was primarily

White Eagles Mardi Gras Indian gang on the Riverboat *President,* 1983   2236/6

11

a celebration of, say, Irish culture. But since black culture is its nucleus, we do feel justified in insisting that the black community be involved on every level."

In addition to expanding black representation among the festival staff and board, the board monitors the festival's production budget. "That financial review is very important," Dent says, "and it's also quite controversial." Furthermore, a series of free educational workshops has been initiated in New Orleans' public schools, featuring renowned musicians who come to town to perform at the festival. Besides this program, free and reduced-price tickets are made available so that the Jazz Fest is accessible to people of all income brackets. To involve more local musicians, smaller-scale events and jam sessions have been added. Held at neighborhood venues, such sets augment the schedule of big-name evening concerts.

These and other matters are closely scrutinized by both the festival staff and the board. "I feel," Dent says, "that we on the board have helped the festival prosper, though we're not always seen that way. The board's broad community spectrum keeps the festival's producers receptive to community interests. If the festival were run solely by the community, without the professional expertise of the producers, then it would probably splinter and go off the deep end. But without the board's community input, George Wein's festival here would probably look just like all his other festivals around the world. We are also trying to involve the community through funding and upgrading the radio station WWOZ, and through the new jazz school which we've established — the Heritage School of Music, under the direction of Edward ('Kidd') Jordan."

Charlie Bering, who joined the staff in 1978 as a jazz producer, has been an important contributor in implementing these changes. "The workshop program, for one, has really flourished," Bering says with pride. "Badi Murphy is running it now, and doing a fine job.

"We want to embrace the whole community," Bering continues, "to use and present all styles of music — modern jazz, Cajun and Zydeco, Gospel, Latin. We were thrown a little when the Riverboat *President* left town in 1988; at first that was devastating. New Orleans is always associated with the river, and boat concerts were a festival highlight for lots of people. But the new River Tent, which replaced the *President,* at least temporarily, gives us the opportunity to make more money. That means more revenue for the Foundation's grant program, and more funding for the local arts community.

"What impressed me so much about the first Jazz Fest I attended," Bering says, " — back in the old days, at Congo Square — was the interaction of the people. The crowd had such a feeling of pleasure and peace, with such a mixture of ages and races. Everybody was celebrating the music. I had just moved to New Orleans, and thought of it as a hardcore racist Southern city. I saw what music could do for people, and I thought, 'This festival is where I belong.'"

This spiritual aspect of the Jazz Fest is also manifested in one of its more unique programming features — the Gospel Tent. Sherman Washington, leader of the Zion Harmonizers, has been involved since the very beginning. "We sang on the first festival at Congo Square," Washington says, "and then when they moved out to the Fair Grounds, Quint asked me to run the Gospel Tent for him. At first I had some trouble with some ministers, because blues was played there — some people call it the Devil's music — and because alcohol was served, too. But now they're with me." Washington, unlike many Gospel singers, is not philosophically opposed to secular music, or the blues in particular. "Music's what's in the heart," he says. "People sing and play the blues 'cause they do it for a living. Some church people don't have a good heart. The way your heart carries you, it'll show up in the way that you carry yourself, with your attitude.

"Yeah, *now* those ministers are with me," Washington repeats, with a preacher's emphasis. "A lot of the groups get happy and don't want to get down off the stage. It's wonderful. I'm proud of the festival. See, they didn't have to think about having a Gospel Tent. They could have gone on without one, but Quint said he had it in his mind, and that dream came true."

Moving from the sublime to the sensational, there seems to be an undisputed consensus as to the festival's most unforgettable character: Bongo Joe. This San Antonio-based street musician, whose real name is George Coleman, plays a variety of homemade percussion instruments, and accompanies himself with hilarious improvised monologues. The result is intriguing, brilliantly original music, with strong links to the West African griot tradition. Coleman's self-titled album, on Arhoolie Records, is a full-strength dose of creativity and eccentric charm. In person, his impact is nothing short of riveting.

Bongo Joe from San Antonio on oil drums, 1972   711/6

"Bongo Joe is six-three, 230 pounds," Quint Davis explains, "and he used to wear a purple fez, Hawaiian shirts with suspenders, Bermuda shorts, and paratrooper boots. He also had an axe in his belt, because he 'tuned' the fifty-five-gallon drums that he played by whacking big holes in them. The first time he played here he insisted on staying at the Fairmont, because in the old days when it was segregated he had been turned away there. I drove him over and besides wearing the whole outfit I just described, he was carrying a suitcase with two speakers embedded in it, pointing outwards. On the inside was a tape recorder, cued up with a tape of hysterical laughter. We'd be stopped at lights and he'd point the suitcase at people on the street and hit 'em with the hysterical laughter, and it was loud, too.

"So we arrive at the Fairmont, where a six-foot-three guy with a fez, Bermuda shorts, paratrooper boots, and an axe in his belt naturally attracted some attention. And when people stared at him, he'd hit 'em with the hysterical laughter tape. You can imagine the reaction."

Lloyd Cottingim, who coordinates the Jazz Fest's musicians' drivers, remembers that "I picked up Bongo Joe at the airport. According to my instructions, he was a 'steel drummer.' But when I got there, he had no instruments with him. I said, 'Did you forget something?' and he said, 'No, but we have to stop by a junkyard.' Well as a driver, I get all kinds of requests: 'Find me a chiropractor, a masseuse, an astrologist, a liquor store, whatever. . . .' So I said, 'No problem, what particular kind of junkyard do you want?' He said he needed barrels. So we went out to this place on Airline Highway where the fence is made out of barrels stacked eight feet high, and to Bongo Joe this place looked just like Werlein's. He bought three or four fifty-five-gallon barrels, still dripping with oil — today I'd probably need an EPA permit to haul them — and off we went.

"That's the kind of stuff," Cottingim explains, "that makes me a festaholic. Doing this crazy job is my opportunity to pay back some of my dues to New Orleans music, to my heritage, my heroes, the things that I grew up with. Plus, the festival is a huge gathering of the tribe — not just the music community, but all of the different people of New Orleans. I'm honored and thrilled to be with the festival, and I'll hang with it as long as it hangs with me."

Rahsaan Roland Kirk with the Herbie Mann band, Ron Burton on keyboard, 1973   852/12

Another unforgettable character in festival reminiscence is the late James Booker III — New Orleans' most talented rhythm and blues pianist, and a major influence on the likes of Henry Butler, Dr. John, and Harry Connick, Jr. "You never knew what Booker would do next," says Joanne Schmidt, a former associate producer. "There was one day, around 1980 maybe, that was really wild. First, this lady shows up at the office in a white uniform, and says that she's a nurse from a health insurance company, and that she's there to give Charlie Bering a physical. I told her to have a seat. Then Ironing Board Sam, this wild piano player, shows up. He was wearing skintight purple lamé pants with no underwear, and they were very revealing, if you catch my drift. He also had on black, high-heel knee boots, no shirt, and a necklace with an electrical plug on the end, painted gold, and gold letters which spelled out the words 'sex plug.' He took a seat next to the nurse, and she was freaking out.

"Then Booker came in, in an absolute tizzy, and told me he had to use my typewriter immediately, to write his will. I said, 'James, I have work to do, can

14

you wait awhile?' but he insisted. So he types out his will, with a clause that upon his death, Aretha Franklin must be notified. Ironing Board Sam and the nurse signed it as witnesses, and he split."

"Booker had a million nicknames for himself," Quint Davis recalls, ". . . 'the Piano Prince,' 'the Piano Pope,' and 'the Emperor of the Ivories.'" At the 1978 gig pictured here, Booker added another monicker when he introduced himself to the crowd as "Eartha Kitt."

"Now one of my most touching memories of the festival," recalls Associate Producer Doratha ("Dodie") Smith-Simmons, "is of Rahsaan Roland Kirk. Even though he was an avant-garde player, he loved traditional jazz. He would go to the Jazz Museum, and stand there holding George Lewis's clarinet, meditating over it. I ended up taking him to a jazz funeral, and even though he was blind, he was filled with the spirit of it, and it was a really emotional thing for him. When he jammed with the Olympia Brass Band at the festival it was a very spiritual moment."

In a more serious vein, Smith-Simmons focusses on some of the problems which have accompanied the Jazz Fest's tremendous growth. "I think that in some ways the festival has gotten too big and too commercial. I would like to see more emphasis in going out and finding more people like Bongo Joe, or the Como Fife and Drum Corps. The rise in ticket prices tends to discourage attendance from the black community — you really don't see a lot of black people out there, except for the last Sunday. I also think that there still needs to be more black involvement in terms of staff. If there were more intern programs going on now, there wouldn't be some of the bad feeling in the black community which exists now."

Such sentiments have led, in the past, to confrontations. Writer/editor/producer Kalamu ya Salaam, the former executive director of the Jazz & Heritage Foundation, recalls that "in the mid-seventies, a group of us in the black community were growing increasingly upset because of the way that the festival was structured. We were being excluded from participation, and there was no channel for improving the situation. We formed a direct-action organization called the African-American Coalition. We told the festival that we were going to disrupt it with a boycott, if we didn't get more black staff members and board members, and more black vendors at the Heritage Fair. As a result, significant changes were made. One was the implementation of the Koindu stage and crafts area for black artists, which is now known as Congo Square."

"George Wein deserves credit," Tom Dent comments, "for his quick response to that situation. He definitely rolled with the punches."

Turning to another controversial issue, Allison Miner comments that "I don't see why the festival needs to bring in big names to draw crowds. Somewhere in the superstar element, the original mission gets lost." "The big names don't really have anything to do with what the festival's about," Dodie Smith-Simmons concurs. "We're getting away from highlighting local talent, which is really what people come to New Orleans to see."

"I have very mixed feelings there," George Wein once told journalist Ashley Kahn. "Remember, I have to draw crowds, so I try to find a certain sense of quality in the people that I use. More than that, I try to find artists who have respect for what we do." Yet another problem is overcrowding, especially at performances by popular artists like the Neville Brothers, B. B. King, or Fats Domino.

"You always have different aesthetics within a community," Quint Davis says, philosophically, "and everybody wants more of what they like. We have a lot of all of it, and we're happy about that. The Jazz Fest's basic spirit has been maintained despite physical changes. We do have a larger profile in terms of guest celebrities, but those artists are keepers of the flame — they're part of the heritage of jazz and American music. I definitely feel that we still make the artistic point that we set out to make."

That artistic point has been underscored over the years by some truly memorable performances. In 1983, for instance, the Rev. Al Green and band arrived late for their set. They ran on stage and started out at full-strength fever pitch, yet the energy somehow kept building. By the end of the show Green had flung away his shirt, and held a single note while spinning like a dervish, his mouth passing in range of the microphone every few seconds. The crowd was mesmerized, at first, and then went wild.

"Stevie Wonder sitting in with the Meters, in '73 — now that was a great one," Quint Davis recalls, looking through Michael Smith's photos. "Then there was Alice May Victor, the first year, playing an upright piano in the grass — the birth of the Gospel Tent! . . . Doug Kershaw — in the early days, he'd bring his mother, and she'd sit on stage during his set. We'd put a box of crawfish on stage, and he'd throw 'em into the crowd. Allen Toussaint . . . for years his riverboat gigs were practically the only appearances he'd make all year, and that really helped make the festival special. Prior to that he had sort of been the Quincy Jones of New Orleans, a reclusive producer. Allen's lending himself to the festival was important in our growing credibility, and I think that it was important for him in stepping out as a performer, too. And let's not forget Irma Thomas's set at the Fair Grounds in 1975 — that marked our first big jump in the size of our audience.

"Now the greatest jam that we ever had," Davis states, "was in 1973. Zigaboo and George Porter, Jr., from the Meters were the rhythm section. Professor Longhair and Roosevelt Sykes both played piano, and they of course were two of the festival's most important heroes. B. B. King was playing guitar, and so was his cousin Bukka White, one of the great old-time country bluesmen. That was the most cosmic set I ever saw in my life."

And, finally, there's *New Orleans Jazz Fest*'s most graphic image — the infamous tattoo. "That's the most unique and important piece of Professor Longhair art in the world," Davis concludes decisively. "It's taken from a photo by Barry Kaiser, and it's on the hip of a woman named Marjorie Knight, who lives in Maui. God bless Marjorie — and God bless Professor Longhair!"

When such fond memories are set aside temporarily, a long hard look into the future reveals on-going growing pains, and significant issues which the festival must continue to address. Still, the festival remains grounded in grass-roots integrity, and energized by the devotion of its staff, performers, and huge audience. Its external appearance may change in the future, making the photos which appear here a vital historical document. But the spiritual core of the Jazz Fest is based in a mood of cultural celebration which blossomed in New Orleans in the late sixties. That sentiment — so graphically captured in these pages — is apt to flourish for many years to come.

BEN SANDMEL

Walter King, B. B. King, and Leon Warren,
1988   2695/35

Acknowledgments

The most difficult problem in producing this book was the choice of images to include. The images were selected out of a stock of more than 14,000 images, and edited down from more than 800 prints. The choices were brutal. Letting this book go to press has been very difficult because even with its over 400 photographs jam-packed with musicians, I was well aware of how many more thousands of musicians who played at the festival are not to be found in these pages. We hope that eventually all musicians who have participated will receive their due credit.

The second most difficult problem for me in producing this book was the photograph identifications. Who is that young lady dancing on stage with Uganda's Drum Troupe in 1974, or that trumpet player behind Earl Turbinton in B. B. King's band in 1972, or all those other women with Willie Bee in the gospel group from Prentiss, Mississippi in 1973? And what do you do when you have three different "authorities" disagreeing about the identification of some musician in the background section of a photograph, slightly out of focus, whose face is partly obscured by an instrument? And in those cases which cannot be clearly resolved do you put a question mark or leave the picture out?

In some cases we were obliged to trust a single source, but in most cases, where there was any question whatsoever, musicians were identified by several sources. If there was still uncertainty about anyone in a picture, we opted simply to identify the featured star.

The Jazz and Heritage Festival staff has been an invaluable source of information and help in identifying the performers and others included in the photographs. For help in identifications we would like to thank Quint Davis, Anna Zimmerman, Nancy Ochsenschlager, Dodie Smith-Simmons, Sally Gates Cobb, Charlie Bering, Sherman Washington, Allison Miner, and others at the festival office. And from the music community we thank Dick Allen, Bruce Raeburn, and Alma Williams at the Hogan Jazz Archives, George Porter, Bruce Macdonald, Jimmy Mack, Milton Batiste, Lars Edegran, James Andrews (Jr. and Sr.), Carl Leblanc, Keith Keller, Clara Joseph, Clive Wilson, Danny Barker, Earl Turbinton, Michael White, Ellis Marsalis, Monk Boudreaux, Lionel Oubichon, Benny

Jones, Irma Thomas, Donald Harrison, Sr., Greg Stafford, "Doc" Paulin, Charmaine Neville, Marc and Ann Savoy, Chris Strachwitz, Steve Armbruster, Pat Jolly, Alton ("Rockin' Dopsie") Rubin, Jeff Fountain, Walter and Jerry Brock, Rosa Lee Hawkins, Allen Fontenot, Michael and David Doucet, Ramsey McLean, and Elliott ("Stackman") Callier, among many others.

Very special thanks are due to all the people who cannot be named here, or who are not pictured herein, who have performed at the festival and/or who contributed over the years in other ways, behind the scenes, to make the festival the wonderful event it is.

For the purpose of subsequent printings and/or updatings of this work we ask that if readers recognize any principal musicians not identified herein, please contact the publisher.

Walking-signboard man, 1975   1310/10

NEW ORLEANS
JAZZ
FEST

Eureka Jazz Band, traditional parade: Booker T. Glass and Anderson Minor (grand marshalls), Earl Humphrey (trombone), Noel ("Papa") Glass (snare drum), Oscar ("Chicken") Henry (trombone), George ("Kid Sheik") Colar (trumpet), Cie Frazier (bass drum), Allan Jaffe (sousaphone), 1970   359/2a

1970-1974

While memories of the 1970 New Orleans Jazz & Heritage Festival are a bit cloudy, and vary to some extent, folks who attended generally recollect that about 350 musicians performed over a period of four days and four nights to about as many "Second-Liners" — people who broke away from their normal schedules to follow the music and celebrate our jazz heritage.

The festival started Wednesday night with the Pete Fountain and Clyde Kerr orchestras for a midnight cruise aboard the side-wheel steamer *President*. On Thursday at noon the Eureka Brass Band began at Canal and Basin streets and gathered crowds for the opening of the first annual Louisiana Heritage Fair in Congo Square (admission $3). Unique Louisiana food, music, and special events continued Thursday, Friday, Saturday, and Sunday from noon until 6 in Congo Square and the Municipal Auditorium.

Strolling among booths offering Grits and Grillades, Shrimp Creole, Crawfish Etouffe, Shrimp and Oyster Gumbo, Chicken Fricassee, Stuffed Bell Peppers, Crabmeat and Shrimp Jambalaya, Creole Succotash, and Begue's Praline Ice Cream, booths offering arts and crafts, and other booths offering all sorts of cultural attractions, patrons could visit music stages presenting everything from Mahalia Jackson to Mardi Gras Indians.

Each night there were special music events in the Auditorium from 8 until midnight — on Thursday night, the Young Tuxedo Brass Band with Sweet Emma, Fats Domino, and others; on Friday night Mahalia Jackson and others; on Saturday night Duke Ellington, Al Hirt, and so on. It was heaven in New Orleans for music lovers.

The first Jazz Fest is generally remembered by those who attended as one of the greatest events in the history of the city. It was a joyous celebration of the city's music and cultural heritage, and the word spread rapidly. But even the festival organizers could never have imagined what would eventually develop from this auspicious beginning.

The second year was even more phenomenal. Also over a period of four days and four nights, and with little organized promotion, the event increased tremendously. People from all over the country came to join in the celebration. Though still relaxed and uncrowded, the second annual New Orleans Jazz & Heritage Festival was such a success that the organizers realized it had already outgrown Congo Square and plans were made to relocate to the Fair Grounds in 1972.

NEW ORLEANS
JAZZ FEST

By 1972 it was clear that the Jazz & Heritage Festival was a "world class" event with giant commercial potential. Over the following years the crowds continued to increase, and more and more entrepreneurs applied to participate. Festival organizers, for their part, were mainly preoccupied with booking the music, accommodating the ever increasing crowds — which always exceeded expectations — and deciding how to select among the growing numbers of art, craft, food, and other concessions people seeking to participate.

As early as 1973 we see the beginning of a resurgence in live music club activity around the city during the Jazz Fest as locals gathered to hear musicians practice for festival appearances.

Food booth: Creole delights, 1970   357/8

Jazz Museum (Justin Winston and friend), 1970   365/32a

Art Gallery: Larry Borenstein (seated), Sandra and Benjamin Jaffe (at right), 1970   365/34a

Mardi Gras Indian jam: the Black Eagles, the Wild Magnolias, and the Golden Eagles, 1970   357/35

Mardi Gras Indian jam: Wild Magnolias, Golden Eagles, and friends, 1970   366/12a

23

Roving hippie dance troupe, 1970   362/6a

Dancers in Congo Square, 1970   360/18a

Eureka Jazz Band: Cie Frazier, Paul Barnes, Oscar ("Chicken") Henry, Terrance Humphrey, Albert Walters, and Percy Humphrey with Mahalia Jackson, 1970   359/15a

Preservation Hall Jazz Band: Percy Humphrey (trumpet), Chester Zardis (bass), Sing Miller (piano), with Woody Allen and Henry Blackburn sitting in, 1970   361/13

Olympia Brass Band jam: Noel ("Papa") Glass (snare drum), Booker T. Glass (bass drum), Allan Jaffe (sousaphone), Harold Dejan (saxophone), Ron Going (clarinet), Percy Humphrey (trumpet), Henry Blackburn (clarinet), 1970   360/13a

Dejan's Olympia Brass Band: Andy Anderson (trumpet), Anderson Minor (grand marshall), Kid Sheik (trumpet), Milton Batiste (trumpet), Noel ("Papa") Glass (snare drum), Harold Dejan (saxophone), Andrew Jefferson (snare drum), Manuel Crusto (clarinet), Booker T. Glass (bass drum), Wendell Eugene (trombone), Homer Eugene (trombone), 1970   365/36a

New Orleans Ragtime Orchestra: Lionel Ferbos (trumpet), Cie Frazier (drums), Orange Kellin (clarinet), Bill Russell (violin), Lars Edegran (piano), James Prevost (bass), Paul Crawford (trombone, not shown), 1970   358/16

BELOW LEFT:
Preservation Hall Jazz Band: Jim Robinson (trombone), Punch Miller (trumpet), John Handy (saxophone), Willie J. Humphrey (clarinet), Narvin Kimbell (banjo), Cie Frazier (drums), George Wein (sitting in on piano), Chester Zardis (bass), 1970   358/34

ABOVE RIGHT:
Pete Fountain Jazz Band (night event): Paul Edwards (drums), Jack Delaney (trombone), Connie Jones (trumpet), Oliver ("Stick") Felix (bass), Pete Fountain (clarinet), and Eddie Miller (tenor sax), 1970   363/23a

Original Tuxedo Brass Band: Waldron C. ("Frog") Joseph (trombone), Jack Willis (trumpet), Joseph ("Cornbread") Thomas (vocals), Frank Fields (bass), Albert ("Papa") French (banjo), 1970   363/32a

Cajun "jam section": Lindsey Bellard (fiddle), Ambrose Thibodeaux (accordion), Morris Ardoin (guitar), Sady Courville (fiddle), 1970   364/14

Cajun jam: Adam Landreneau (fiddle), Sady Courville (fiddle), Boisec Ardoin (accordion), 1970   363/13a

Cyprien and friends: Joe Carpenter (guitar), Adam Landreneau (fiddle), Sady Courville (fiddle), Cyprien Landreneau (accordion), Savy Augustine (triangle), Ambrose Thibodeaux (triangle), 1970   358/2a

Alice May Victor in the Gospel Tent, 1970   362/20a

The Morning Star Baptist Church Choir under the leadership of Sister Annie Pavageaux, 1970   357/26

Dick Allen, Mary Tunis, Susan Cosgrove, with Bob Green on piano, 1970   361/19

Willie Thomas, Percy Randolph, and Babe Stovall, 1970   365/28a

Dizzy Gillespie and Bongo Joe, 1971   540/26

Allen Fontenot & the Country Cajuns: Leroy Veillon (accordion), Darrell Brasseaux (drums), Clarence Vidrine (rhythm guitar), Hudson Dauzat (lead guitar), Allen Fontenot (fiddle), 1971   540/29

"Stage 1": Annie Pavageaux (vocals), with Lars Edegran (piano), Orange Kellin (clarinet), and Rolf Wahl (trumpet), 1971   540/30

Curtis ("Coco Robicheaux") Arceneaux cartoon booth, 1971   540/33

Sister Gertrude Morgan with Jules Cahn on camera,
1972   709/8

"Mixed media": food and crafts area, 1972   720/2

Whole Food Company booth, 1972   724/34

Como Fife and Drum Corps: Napoleon Strickland (fife), Othar and Bernice Turner (snare drums), R. L. Boyce (bass drum), 1972   724/36

Fairview Baptist Church Band: Morris Combs (trumpet), Leroy Jones (trumpet), Joe Torregano (clarinet), Gene Mims (clarinet), Greg Stafford (trumpet), 1972   724/17

Guitar Kelly and Silas Hogan, 1972   708/3

Sonny Stitt and Ellis Marsalis, 1972   720/17

AT LEFT:

Olympia Brass Band: Anderson Minor (grand marshall), Paul Crawford (trombone), Harold Dejan (saxophone), William Grant Brown (sousaphone), Reginald Koeller (trumpet), Richard ("King") Matthews (grand marshall), Gerald Joseph (trombone), and Booker T. Glass (grand marshall), 1972   720/11

AT LEFT:
Snooks Eaglin and Henry Roeland Byrd (a.k.a. Professor Longhair), 1972   711/17

B. B. King, 1972   721/32

Clifton and Cleveland Chenier, 1972   714/34

Clifton Chenier band on stage 3, 1972
722/18a

40

Former governor Jimmie Davis with the Meyers Brothers band and the Season Travelers with Hubert
Davis, 1972   722/6a

Stage 4 overview: Wild Magnolias and Golden Eagles Mardi Gras Indian gangs, 1972   724/37

Paul Barnes, Percy Humphrey, and Clement Tervalon, 1972   706/16

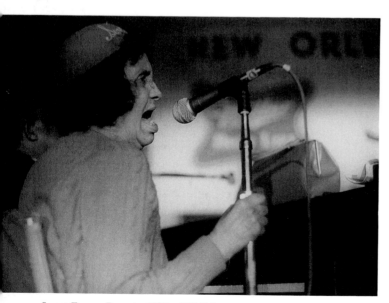

Sweet Emma Barrett, 1972   706/36

Al McKibbon, Art Blakey, Dizzy Gillespie, and Sonny Stitt,
1972   710/32

Kai Winding (trombone), Dizzy Gillespie (trumpet), Sonny Stitt (sax), Al McKibbon (bass), and
Thelonious Monk (keyboard), 1972   711/22

B. B. King and band, 1972   715/22a

Nina Simone at a night event, 1972   719/22a

Sady Courville, 1972   726/1a

Como Fife and Drum Corps: Napoleon Strickland (fife), Bernice Turner (drum), R. L. Boyce (bass drum), Othar Turner (drum), 1973   824/17a

Como Fife and Drum Corps: Napoleon Strickland (fife), R. L. Boyce (drum), Bernice Turner (bass drum), and Othar Turner (drum), 1973   856/24a

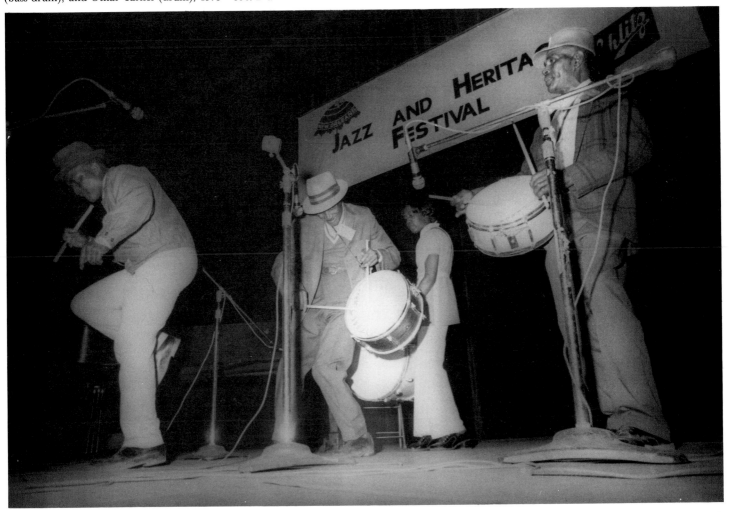

Sister Gertrude Morgan, 1973   851/17

Sister Gertrude Morgan and Sacha Borenstein, 1973   835/19a

46

The new Louisiana Heritage Fair banner,
1973 826/28

Buster Holmes' red beans booth, 1973 832/7

Crafts, 1973 825/3

The Meters: Leo Nocentelli, George Porter, Art Neville, 1973   836/32

Percussion jam on the infield: Uganda's Drum Troupe with Alfred ("Uganda") Roberts, 1973   833/21

Stevie Wonder with the Meters, 1973   836/16

Presentation of Michael P. Smith photo of B. B. King to
B. B. King (with Quint Davis), 1973   838/13

Professor Longhair (piano), George Porter (bass), Joseph
("Zigaboo") Modeliste (drums), and Snooks Eaglin (guitar),
1973   848/4a

Roosevelt Sykes, B. B. King (guitar), Bukka White (guitar), George Porter (bass), Professor Longhair (piano), 1973   845/34

Howlin' Wolf, 1973   856/10a

Taj Mahal, 1973   844/10a

Pete Fountain orchestra on the Riverboat *President*: Jack Delaney (trombone), Charlie Lodice (drums), Connie Jones (trumpet), ? (trumpet), Pete Fountain (clarinet), Oliver ("Stick") Felix (bass), Eddie Miller (saxophone), Earl Viouvich (piano), 1973   829/28

Dave Brubeck, 1973   850/19a

Dejan's Olympia Brass Band with Rahsaan Roland Kirk: Gerald Joseph (trombone), Allan Jaffe
(sousaphone), Noel ("Papa") Glass (drum), William Brown (tuba), Roland Kirk (horns), Joseph
Torregano (trumpet), Milton Batiste (trumpet), Edmond Foucher (trumpet), with Richard ("King")
Matthews, Fats Houston, and Anderson Minor as grand marshalls, 1973   830/15

Second-line parade: Homer Eugene on trombone; Danny Barker and Henry Dudley as grand marshalls, 1973   858/32a

Eddie Bo, 1973   831/14

Willie Bee and her gospel group from Prentiss, Mississippi, 1973   822/30a

Canray Fontenot and Boisec Ardoin, 1973   832/30

Allen Fontenot and the Country Cajuns (on Thursday!): Clarence Vidrine (guitar), Allen Fontenot (fiddle), Darrell Brasseaux (drums), Joe Young (accordion), Hudson Dauzat (guitar), 1973   823/12a

Bukka White, 1973   823/31a

Larry Pannia (drums), "Willie Tee" (Wilson Turbinton, keyboard), Earl Turbinton (sax), and Julius Farmer (bass), 1973   837/25

Jazz at the Fair Grounds: Tom Ebbert (trombone), Clive Wilson (trumpet), Percy ("Butz") Massicot (drums), Johnny Wiggs (cornet), and Raymond Burke (clarinet), 1973   832/8

Early live music club activity: George Davis, Johnny Vidacovich, Earl Turbinton, and Julius Farmer at Lu & Charlie's, 1973   860/9

Crowd in front of Benny Spellman's stage, 1974   1125/8

Snooks Eaglin on stage 2, 1974   1138/16

Crafts, 1974   1135/32a

Traditional jazz parade: Freddie Lonzo (trombone), Jerry Greene (tuba), Wendell Eugene (trombone), with Danny Barker (grand marshall) for the Onward Brass Band, 1974   1127/13

Jazz parade with the Olympia Brass Band: Kid Sheik (trumpet), Emmanuel Paul (saxophone), Noel ("Papa") Glass (bass drum), 1974   1147/32a

Earl ("Fatha") Hines, 1974   1130/15

Presentation of a plaque to Earl Hines, 1974   1130/27

Herbie Hancock with Paul Jackson on bass, 1974
1128/9a

Yusef Lateef, 1974   1126/31

Kid Thomas Valentine Jazz Band: Wendell Eugene (trombone), Kid Thomas (trumpet), Emmanuel
Paul (saxophone), Alonzo Stewart (drums), 1974   1142/1a

Benny Spellman going into the crowd, 1974   1139/35

Benny Spellman, 1974   1139/17

Art Neville, the Meters, 1974   1140/27a

The Meters: Zigaboo Modeliste (drums),
George Porter (bass), and Leo Nocentelli
(guitar), 1974   1140/3a

The Meters with Uganda Roberts, 1974
1140/10

Jam on the infield: Uganda's Drum Troupe, 1974   1127/3

Uganda's Drum Troupe with Uganda Roberts   1138/26

Sady Courville and friends: Sady Courville (fiddle), Dennis McGee (fiddle), Nathan Abshire (accordion), Irene Fruge, Preston Manuel (guitar), 1974   1135/17a

Clifton Chenier, 1974   1141/25a

Barry Martyn's Legends of Jazz: Joe Darrensberg (clarinet), Alton Purnell (piano), Andrew Blakeney (trumpet), Louis Nelson (trombone), and Barry Martyn (drums, not shown), 1974   1133/27a

Alvin Batiste conducting the Jaguar Jazz Ensemble from Southern University of New Orleans, 1974   1133/10a

New Orleans jazz: Wendell Eugene (trombone), Placide Adams (bass), Don Albert (trumpet), Freddie Kohlman (drums), Walter Lewis (keyboard), and Louis Cottrell (clarinet), 1974   1133/16a

Society Jazz Band and friends: Johnson McRee (vocals), Percy Massicot (drums), ? (trombone), Chink Martin (bass), Clive Wilson (trumpet), Johnny Wiggs (trumpet), Les Muscutt (banjo), Raymond Burke (clarinet), Jeff Riddick (piano), 1974   1138/32

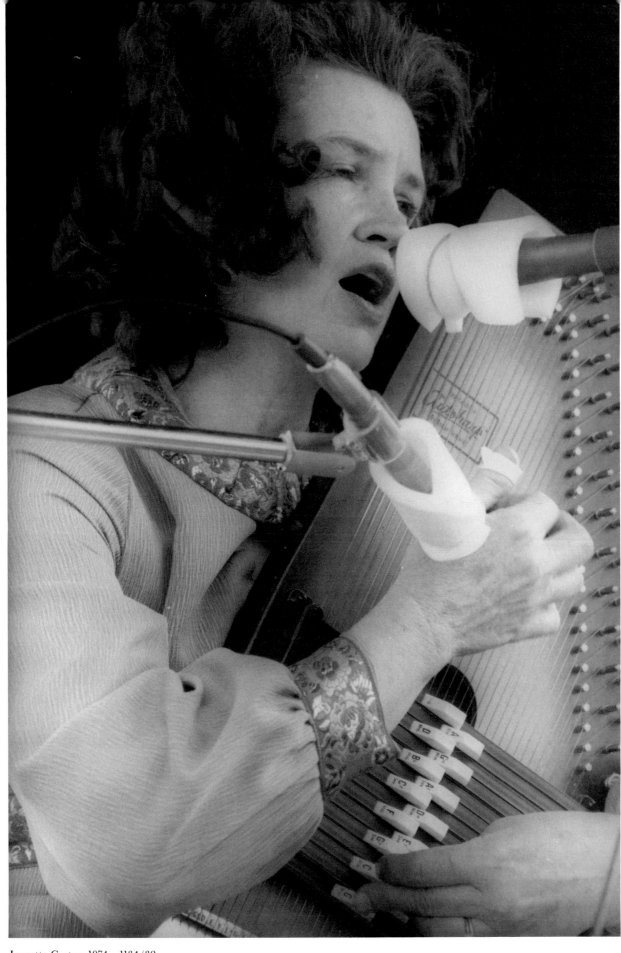

Jeanette Carter, 1974   1134/32

Lightnin' Hopkins, 1974 1136/12a

Tuts Washington, 1974 1146/9a

Robert Pete Williams, 1974   1139/6

71

Welcome to the Louisiana Heritage Fair sign, 1975   1304/19a

1975–1979

The New Orleans Jazz & Heritage Festival is indeed unique. Because of its location in New Orleans, and its interrelationship with the city, it has an ambience and character that is singular among all the great music festivals in the world. The photographs presented here reflect an amazing growth — the actual development of a world class event in just a few short years.

By 1975 one has only to look at the entrance banner and the crowds streaming into the Fair Grounds on the opening day of that year to know that the Jazz Fest was here to stay.

In 1976 the festival expanded to include two weekends to take advantage of its phenomenal popularity. It was held April 9 through 18 of that year. Gradually, over the following years, music clubs and restaurants in the city geared up during the Jazz Fest to accommodate the large numbers of visitors who remained in town between the two weekends to explore more fully the living cultural resources of the city and surrounding region. Small businesses in the city benefitted extraordinarily — especially businesses and cultural attractions being featured at the festival. The Jazz Fest was clearly the agent for a rapidly increasing recognition of south Louisiana music and culture.

Already, by this time, New Orleans' music industry was showing signs of revival. It was during this period, for example, that a small group of local music lovers, several who had been involved with the Jazz Fest (including myself), were inspired to combine their resources to found a music club called Tipitina's — a live music club to provide a home for real New Orleans music all year around. The founders of Tipitina's were concerned that our best musicians were leaving the city because they had so few places to play during the rest of the year.

During the latter half of the 1970s, various groups and individuals became concerned about the amount of economic development at the festival, and began work to ensure that the New Orleans "music family" would remain a primary beneficiary of the burgeoning event. Consequently a struggle developed between the black and white "societies" involved. Although the festival was already organized as a nonprofit venture, the black group pointed out that most of the musicians were black and most of the audience and management were white, and that the benefits of the festival were accruing in a disproportionate manner to the advantage of white society. These points were well taken and in the following years a combined group worked to ensure that the character of the New Orleans

NEW ORLEANS JAZZ FEST

Jazz & Heritage Festival would remain true to New Orleans, that profits deriving from this event would be distributed fairly within the traditional music and crafts communities without favoring any particular ethnic or cultural group.

The manner in which this issue was resolved at the festival was exemplary, and though these sorts of deliberations have not always been easy, it can be said that in spite of some very understandable frictions the Jazz Fest has served to unite New Orleans more than any other event in the city's history.

In 1979, to celebrate its tenth anniversary, the festival was presented over three weekends (April 20–May 6), and the highly popular African Market Place (formerly Koindu Village, now Congo Square) was established.

James Carroll Booker III ("Music Magnifico," piano), Emmanuel Morris (bass), "Alto Red" Morgan (saxophone), Bernard ("Bunchy") Johnson (drums), 1975   1305/19a

Earl King, 1975   1306/4

Crowd at Chocolate Milk stage, 1975   1307/8a

Irma Thomas, Julian Vaught on saxophone, 1975   1315/5

Earl Turbinton (saxophone) with Willie Tee (keyboard), 1975   1317/8

Young Men Olympian Social & Pleasure Club parade with "Ghost" as grand marshall, 1975   1306/7

Bruce Brice at the Folk Heritage Village,
1975   1314/21

Craft Village, 1975   1316/30a

Carlos Sanchez, 1975   1308/21a

Dick Richard (steel guitar), "T-neg" Gaspard (drums), Lionel LeLeux (fiddle), Marc Savoy (accordion), D. L. Menard (guitar), 1975   1314/19

Flamenco dancers with Carlos Sanchez, 1975   1308/33a

Freddie Hubbard, 1975   1312/35a

Scene Boosters Social & Pleasure Club parade, 1976   1370/12a

Water supply, 1976   1376/15

Bo Dollis, Big Chief of the Wild Magnolias, going into crowd giving feathers, 1976   1373/15a

Bo Dollis (right) and Monk Boudreaux, Big Chief of the Golden Eagles, 1976   1373/29a

Crowd shot, 1976   1373/28a

Quint Davis, producer (on right), with
Professor Longhair (center) and friend,
1976 1377/2a

Earl Turbinton (sax) with Professor Longhair, 1976 1377/6a

The Fair, 1976   1376/35

Leroy Jones' Hurricane Brass Band: Anthony
("Tuba Fats") Lacen (tuba), 1976   1376/19

Gospel tent, 1976   1370/7a

AT RIGHT:
Ella Fitzgerald and Stevie Wonder, 1977

Professor Longhair, 1977   1445/31

The Dixie Cups: Rosa Lee Hawkins, Joanne Kennedy (standing in for Beverly Brown), and Barbara Hawkins, 1977   1460/10

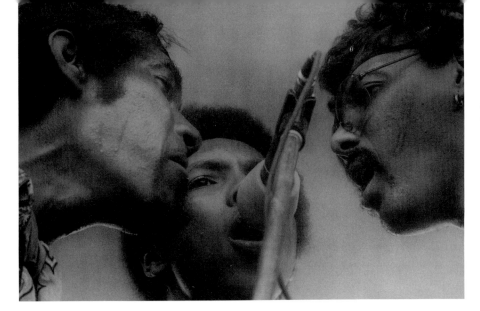

Cyril, Ivan, and Aaron Neville, 1977
1447/22

George ("Big Chief Jolly") Landry of the Wild Tchoupitoulas and Percy ("Big Chief Pete") Lewis of the Black Eagles, 1977   1447/13

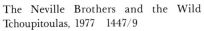

Aaron Neville, 1977   1453/22

The Neville Brothers and the Wild Tchoupitoulas, 1977   1447/9

Washboard Leo (on right) with Cornbread, 1977   1443/9a

Crowd shot, 1977   1448/6

Overview of stage 5, featuring Cornbread, 1977   1466/36a

Ironing Board Sam, 1977   1446/34

John Mooney, 1977   1461/23a

Percy Mayfield, 1977   1453/10

Butch Mudbone, 1977 1454/13

Merle and Doc Watson, 1977 1462/35a

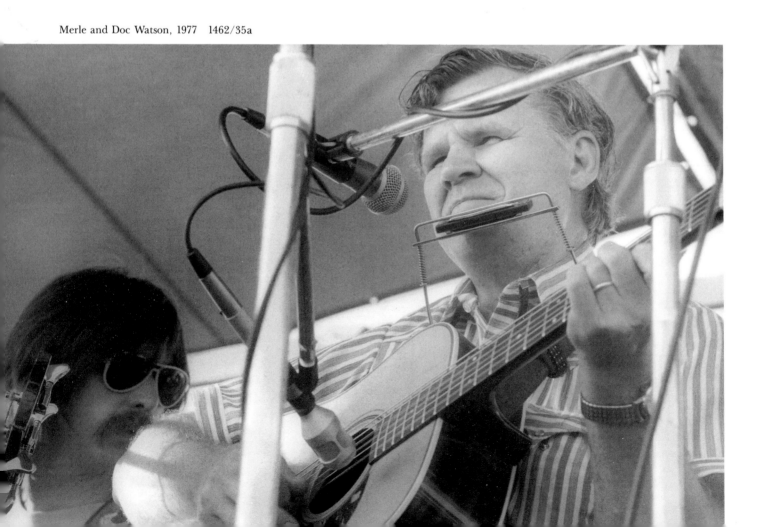

Fair Grounds field play, 1977   1460/19

Bonnie Raitt, 1977   1458/23

Marcel Richardson (keyboard), Walter Washington (guitar and vocals), Thomas Ellis (drums), Byron Johns (clarinet and sax), Elliott William Patrick ("Stackman") Callier (sax), Richard Dixon (bass), 1977 1463/6a

Young Men Olympian Social & Pleasure Club: Steve Soloman (grand marshall), Sherman's Young Tuxedo Brass Band with Aywood Johnson (trombone), Allan Jaffe (tuba), 1977 1459/15a

Bobby ("Blue") Bland, 1977 1449/23a

Crowd, 1978 1616/J3/28a

Stanley John on pans with Professor Longhair, 1978   1612/12

"Brooklyn Robert" Weiner (harmonica),
Uganda Roberts (conga drums), Professor
Longhair (piano), Earl Gorden (drums),
Walter Payton (bass), 1978   1612/35

Fabulous Thunderbirds: Jimmie Lee Vaughan
(guitar), Kim Wilson (vocals), Keith Fergu-
son (bass), 1978   1606/6a

James Booker and Harry Connick, Jr., 1978   1603/8

Oliver Morgan with Melvin Lastie on trumpet and David
Lastie on saxophone, 1978   1613/21

Oliver Morgan joins the audience, 1978   1613/22

Backstage at the Neville Brothers with the
Wild Tchoupitoulas, 1978   1613/30

Cyril Neville (Neville Brothers) and Norman Bell (Second Chief, Wild Tchoupitoulas),
1978   1602/30

B. B. King, 1978   1616/27a

Muddy Waters, 1978   1616/21a

AT RIGHT:
Exuma, 1978   1604/3

Russell Bradshaw ("T-Bone Man") with Nancy Ochsenschlager (Fair Grounds producer), 1978   1605/8a

Dolls at the Craft Village, 1978   1605/3

Lorena B. Langley, Louisiana Indian baskets, 1978   1616/J4/26

Kid City, 1978   1616/J4/14

Zulu Club booth, 1978   1610/31a

Hurricane Brass Band: Ernest Watson (saxophone), Jack Willis (trumpet), Anthony ("Tuba Fats") Lacen (tuba), Frank Naundorf (trombone), 1978   1604/15

The Flora Moulton Group: Tim Lewis (guitar), Flora Moulton (slide guitar), and Larry Wise (mouth harp), 1978   1613/16

Odetta, 1978   1609/28

Bongo lessons with Bongo Joe, 1978   1609/24

John Hawkins with the Zion Harmonizers,
1979 1742/35

William ("Peter") Walker (guitar) and the Mighty Chariots, 1979   1742/29

Mary Davis and Claudia ("the Praline Lady")
Dumestre, 1979   1734/18

Les Blank, filmmaker, at the food booths,
1979   1738/28a

Food booths, 1979   1738/35a

Koindu, 1979   1740/33a

Gentlemen of Leisure, 1979   1743/30

Jazz parade with the Onward Brass Band: Chris Clifton (trumpet), Charles Joseph (trombone), Oscar Rouzan (saxophone), Kirk Joseph (tuba), with Henry Dudley as grand marshall, 1979   1741/9a

Percy ("Pete") Lewis (Big Chief, Black Eagles), Larry Boudreaux (Black Eagles), and Norman Bell (Second Chief, Wild Tchoupitoulas), 1979   1735/16a

Stanley John, Professor Longhair, Eddie Volker, 1979   1744/21

Aaron Neville (cowbell), James Ledet (drums), Jason Neville (cowbell), Leo Nocentelli (guitar), Ivan Neville (tambourine), 1979   1744/11

Voodoo Queen Ava K. Jones with Bo Dollis and the Wild Magnolias Mardi Gras Indian gang at the entrance to the Riverboat *President* night concert, 1979   1739/37

Dew Drop Inn "revisited" at the Contemporary Arts Center: Morris Bashmien (saxophone), Reginald ("Trees") Johnson (bass), Charles Neville (saxophone), Fred Kemp (saxophone), Teddy Riley (guitar), and Charmaine Neville (vocals), 1979   1753/25

Dew Drop Inn "revisited" at the Contemporary Arts Center: Charles Neville (saxophone), Bernard ("Bunchy") Johnson (drums), Fred Kemp (saxophone), Reginald Johnson (bass), Teddy Riley (guitar), Joe ("Mr. Google Eyes") August (vocals), 1979   1753/27

The Balfa Brothers Cajun band: J. W. Pelsia on steel guitar, Dick Richard and Dewey Balfa on fiddle, 1979   1740/22a

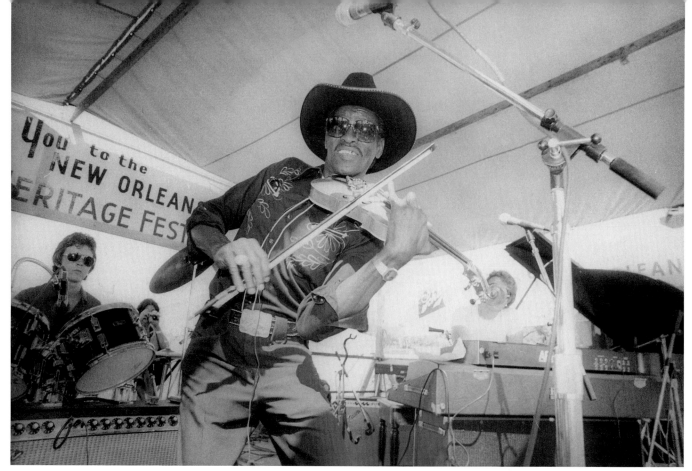

Gatemouth Brown, 1979   1752/7

Etta James, 1979   1743/29a

Staff (partially identified and not always in order): Charlie Bering, Lois Dejean, Badi Murphy, Andy Wallace, Tom Golden, Rhonda Ford, Clifton Webb, Walter Lenk, Nancy Ochsenschlager, Laura Laughlin, Dawn Griffin, Kelly Sullivan, Joanne Schmidt, Anna Zimmerman, Tague Richardson, John Murphy, Sally McPeak, John Phillips, Vitrice McMurray Rankin, Dodie Smith-Simmons, Beth Gasmon, John Schreiber, Coleman Spike Barkin, Steve Solecek, and friends, 1979   1726/11a

Mardi Gras Indian jam: Percy Lewis (Big Chief Pete, Black Eagles), George Landry (Big Chief Jolly, Wild Tchoupitoulas), Charles Taylor (Big Chief, Yellowjackets), Barbara Wallace, and Norman Bell (Second Chief, Wild Tchoupitoulas), 1980   1828/13

Indian second-line percussion by side of stage, 1980   1828/18

1980-1984

By 1980 the effects of the festival on the city were being widely discussed. By this time it had become something like a giant international music trade exposition or convention. The New Orleans Jazz Fest was known as a boundless recreational resource, for its innovative bookings and ingenious combinations and groupings of music and musicians. Along with music lovers and tourists in general, booking agents, producers, recording engineers, radio and TV producers, and other professionals from every area of the music and entertainment industry gathered in New Orleans at this time to scout the latest talent and trade information. For people involved in the music business, New Orleans had become the best place in the world to be during the last weekend of April through the first weekend of May every year.

The reasons for this were many. Aside from all the industry business now being conducted around the festival it was realized that the festival period also provided unique access to little-known treasures of the city. Everybody who came to the festival also came to see New Orleans, to visit local music clubs and record stores, to eat at the fine neighborhood ethnic restaurants, and to visit the legendary ghetto neighborhood live music clubs which were jammed during the Jazz Fest.

It was soon noticed that people attending the Jazz Fest were not patronizing normal tourist venues. Visitors commented that a very particular sort of communication network had developed around the Fest during this two-week period. One could discover the best of what was going on in town — the best new restaurants, the most happening live music clubs, and the cutting edge of whatever else one might be interested in. Producers from Rounder, Arhoolie, or Blacktop Records could always be found at the best new clubs in the city, and Columbia, Concord, CBS, and Warner Brothers were not far behind. During this period, largely through the festival, both professionals and visitors were offered privileged access to the city's inner attractions. Each day's events at the Fair Grounds were only the beginning to one's investigation of the city's music and cultural heritage. In sum, this was the best time of year for anyone to visit New Orleans.

During the 1980s the Jazz Fest developed into an event equal to Mardi Gras in its size and effect on the city. Insiders and outsiders who come almost every year — some for professional purposes and some for their annual vacations — were planning their calendars around the New Orleans Jazz & Heritage Festival. The rewards of the recognition brought to New Orleans music and culture by the Jazz Fest were beginning to be harvested all year around.

Jake Jaeglewitz (traditional alligator art),
1980   1828/5

One Mo' Time (again) in the Jazz Tent: Pud
Brown (clarinet), Lionel Ferbos (trumpet),
John Robichaux (drums), and Barbara
Shorts, Sharon Nabonne, and Sadie Blake
(vocals), 1980   1829/37a

Lionel Hampton, 1980   1829/3a

Byrd family benefit poster booth, sponsored by Sweet Molasses, 1981   1959/27

Running to get in line for the "official" poster,
1981   1949/29a

Stuffed mirliton booth, 1981   1950/22

Daddy Boy with canes in Craft Village, 1981   1949/23a

The Savoy Music Center at the Jazz Fest: Dewey Balfa (fiddle), Marc Savoy (accordion), Ann Allen Savoy (guitar), and friends, 1981   1948/6a

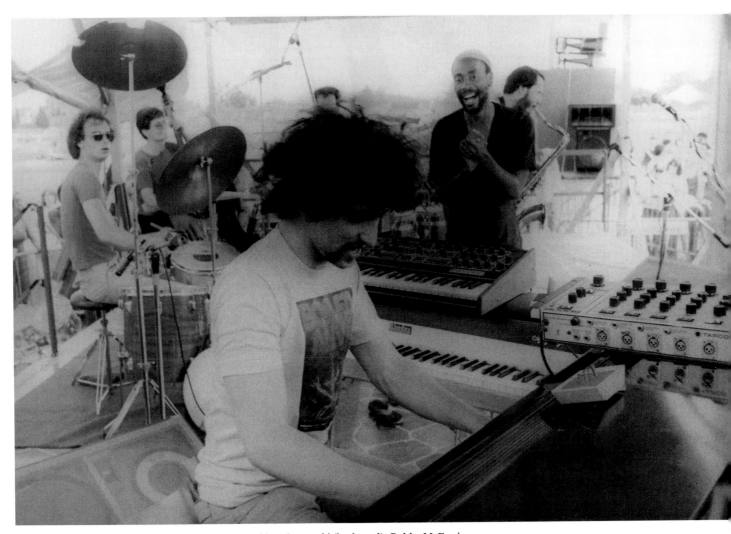

John Vidacovich (drums), Jim Singleton (bass), David Torkanowski (keyboard), Bobby McFerrin (vocals), Tony Dagradi (saxophone), 1981   1955/37a

Neptune Jazz Band from Zimbabwe: Cesar Fratantoni (clarinet), Stephen Fratantoni (trumpet), Daniel Siankope (trombone), Japhet Siankope (drums), Sabrina Siankope (banjo), Trywell Siankope (bass), 1981 1960/19

Coteau reunion: Tommy Comeaux (mandolin), Michael Doucet (fiddle), Kenneth Blevins (drums), Bessyl Duhon (fiddle and accordion), Dana Breaux (guitar), Gary Newman (guitar), Bruce Macdonald (guitar), 1981   1947/9a

Cab Calloway, 1981   1952/5a

Louis Nelson (trombone), Kid Thomas
Valentine (trumpet), 1981   1962/20

Dexter Gordon on the Riverboat, 1981
1955/16a

Buckwheat Zydeco, 1981 1950/17

Cecil Taylor, 1981 1958/12

Irving McLean and group, 1981 1950/10

Cajun jambalaya, 1981   1950/27

Koindu, 1981   1950/34

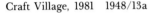

Craft Village, 1981   1948/13a

Narvin Kimbell, 1982   2081/26a

Percy Humphrey, 1982   2081/29a

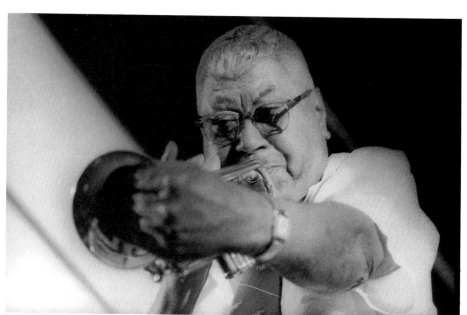

James Prevost, 1982   2082/7

Cie Frazier, 1982   2082/11

Louis Nelson, 1982   2082/13

Dr. Daddy-O (Vernon Winslow), 1982   2081/5a

Bessie Griffin, 1982   2081/13a

Mamou Hour Cajun Band with Sady Courville (fiddle), Roy Fuslier (accordion), and Preston Manuel (guitar), 1982   2070/12

Bruce Daigrepont and Bourre, 1982
2074/7a

AT RIGHT:
James Booker and Harry Connick, Jr.,
1982   2077/36a

Freddie Hubbard, 1982   2083/25

Big Twist, 1982   2074/11a

Allen Toussaint, 1982   2082/33a

122

Stanley Turrentine, 1982   2079/8a

Dr. Michael White (clarinet), Frank Oxley
(drums), 1982   2082/20

James Black, 1982   2077/35

Chuck Berry, 1982   2070/23

Hot air balloon, 1983   2194/33

AT RIGHT:
Professor Gizmo (the one-man band) Rick
Elmore, 1983   2192/31a

Joyce and George Wein (executive producer),
1983   2195/34

Danny Barker (guitar), Louise ("Blue Lu") Barker (vocals),
Greg Stafford (trumpet), Oscar Rouzan (sax), 1983   2190/19

Ernie K-Doe, 1983   2192/25a

Buddy Guy and Jr. Wells, 1983   2194/31

Rufus Thomas, 1983   2199/7

Al Green, 1983   2200/21

Eddie Harris with Johnny Vidacovich on drums, 1983   2194/20

Jim Singleton, 1983   2194/15

Alvin Batiste, 1983   2192/19a

Burning Spear, 1983   2193/11

Dirty Dozen Brass Band: Charles Joseph (trumpet), Kirk Joseph (sousaphone), Gregory Davis (trumpet), Lionel Batiste (bass drum), Jenell Marshall (snare drum), Kevin Harris (tenor sax), Roger Lewis (baritone and soprano sax), 1983   2192/11a

Roy Orbison, 1983   2190/14

Gerald ("Jake") Millon, Big Chief, and the
White Eagles Mardi Gras Indian gang at the
Fair Grounds, 1983   2197/13

Big Joe Turner, 1983   2190/23

AT RIGHT:
Brother Percy Randolph, 1983   2194/23

Crowd, 1984   2307/35

Production crew (partially identified): Ben Sandmel, Charlie Bering, Sandra Blair Richardson, Ifama Arsan, Rhonda Ford, Reggie Houston, Laura Laughlin, Stephanie Samuel, Kelly Sullivan, Camille Hardy, Nancy Ochsenschlager, Dee Lindsey, Quint Davis, Sherman Washington, Linda Berry, Dawn Griffin, Anna Zimmerman, Dodie Smith-Simmons, Tague Richardson, Eddie Lambert, Connie Wessels, Vicky Bell, Jimmy McEntel, Otto Campo, 1984   2296/23

WWOZ Tent: Jerry Brock interview with the feet (tap dance) of Buster Andrews, Sidney Hill, and Darnell Andrews, 1984   2302/22a

WWOZ Jerry Brock interview with Danny Barker, 1984   2305/23a

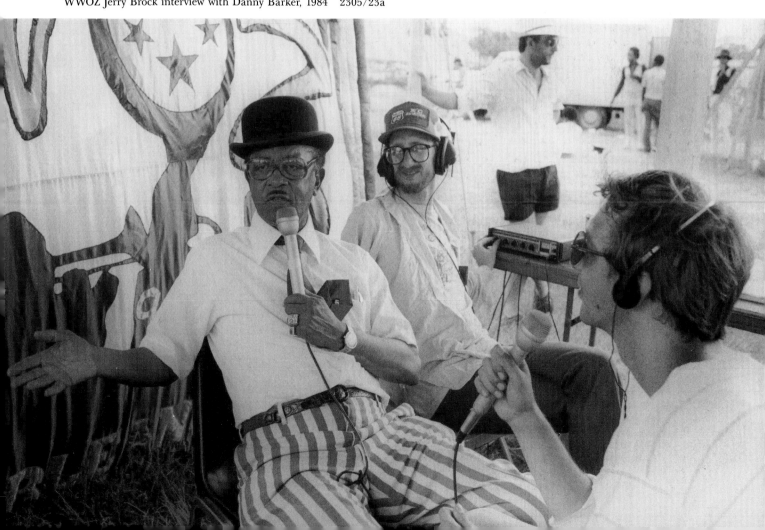

Ivan Neville with the Neville Brothers, 1984   2307/33

"Deacon John" Moore (guitar) and Charles Moore (bass), 1984   2310/26

Linda Hopkins, 1984   2301/26

Narvin Kimbell, 1984   2308/17

Willie Humphrey, 1984   2308/22

Frank Parker, 1984   2308/28

Wayne Bennett, 1984   2306/7

Sonny Rollins, 1984   2300/16

Joe Newman, 1984   2310/8

Bill Monroe, 1984   2307/20

Young Tuxedo Brass Band: John Simmons (trumpet), Greg Stafford (trumpet), Laurence Batiste
(snare drum), 1985   2386/24a

1985–

In reviewing the life of the Jazz Fest from 1985 to the present it's interesting to compare recent festivals to those held in Congo Square and the Municipal Auditorium in 1970 and 1971. Some people nostalgically recall the two festivals in Congo Square as being the most wonderful of all. Those two events are recollected as veritable wonderlands of New Orleans music and culture. After just two years the festival had grown so large it had to be moved to the Fair Grounds...this after only eight days and nights of presentation in two years!

In recent years the festival at the Fair Grounds has assumed the profile of a small but crowded city, with most of the attendant problems. The crowds today are almost oppressive. It is a testimony to the extreme high quality of the event and intelligent management, on the part of both the festival and the city, that the festival has remained such a wonderful and beneficial celebration.

The Jazz Fest, in fact, has opened a new window on the world of music and cultural heritage in New Orleans. Aside from providing quality recreation for hundreds of thousands of our citizens, and millions of visitors, the Jazz Fest has greatly increased awareness around the world of the roots of New Orleans music and culture. Even more importantly, both at home and around the world there is a growing recognition of the tremendous value of our unique living cultural heritage.

The New Orleans Jazz & Heritage Festival is more than twenty years old now, reaching adulthood. We should think of this event as exemplifying what can be achieved from mature presentation and coordinated promotion of our music and multicultural heritage. There is much to learn from taking a closer look at this singular event — and the city which produced it.

Food, 1985 2383/36

Franklin Avenue Baptist Church Choir,
1985 2379/22a

WWOZ interview: Vernon ("Duke-a-
Paducah") Dugas, Billy Dell, Oliver Morgan,
Mac ("Dr. John") Rebennack, Jessie Hill,
1985 2376/11

AT RIGHT:
Lionel Oubichon "Bird" witch doctor, White
Eagles, 1985 2378/13

The Dixie Cups with Aaron Neville: Rosa Lee Hawkins, Dale Thomas-Mickle, Aaron Neville, and Barbara Hawkins, 1985   2373/29a

Leslie Smith with ? Jackson and local attorney Elliot Snellings, 1985   2373/18a

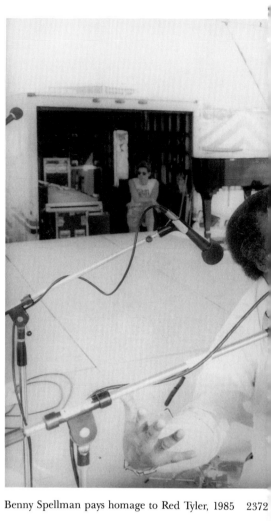

Benny Spellman pays homage to Red Tyler, 1985   2372

Chris Owens, 1985   2373/8a

lero (bass), 1985   2381/28

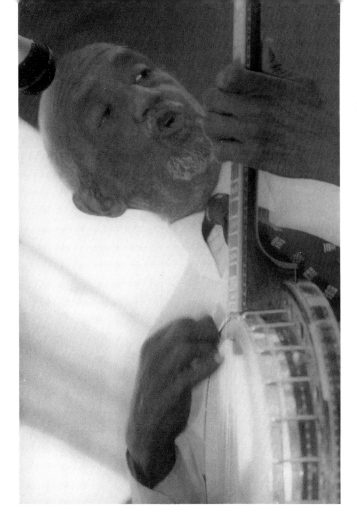

Emmanuel Sayles, 1985   2383/5a

Sippie Wallace, 1985   2375/20

Art Neville with the Staple Singers, 1985   2372/26

Rockin' Sidney, 1985   2375/4

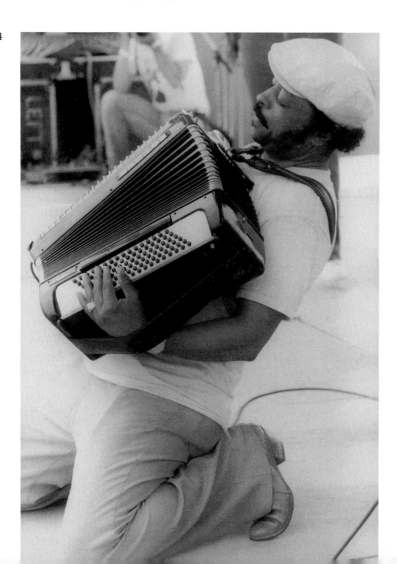

Obey and his Interreformers band, 1986   2462/28

Chief Commander Ebenizer Obey, 1986
2462/8

Crowd, 1986   2466/8a

The Avenue Steppers and Treme Sports marching clubs: Joe Bernard (grand marshall), with the Tornado Brass Band (Anthony Lacen, tuba; George Johnson, trumpet; Michael Johnson, trombone), 1986 2459/37

Jam on the infield, 1986 2460/13a

Scene Boosters second-line parade, 1986 2463/15a

Dodie Smith-Simmons, Odetta, Sandra Jaffe, Joyce Wein, 1986   2459/33

Staff: Quint Davis, Nancy Ochsenschlager,
Kelly Sullivan, 1986   2458/30

Olympia Brass Band (WWOZ radio interview): Ernest Watson (baritone sax), Frank Naundorf
(trombone), Gerald Joseph (trombone), Noel ("Papa") Glass (drum), 1986   2463/18a

Original New Orleans Buckjumpers Social and Pleasure Club with Doc Paulin's Brass Band: Scott Paulin (trombone), Edward Reed (saxophone), Ernest ("Doc") Paulin (trumpet), Ricky Paulin (trumpet), Dwayne Paulin (tuba), Phillip Paulin (saxophone), Julius Lewis (saxophone), Kenneth Maxwell (trombone), with Waldorf ("Gip") Gibson, grand marshall for the Young Men Olympian marching club, 5th division, 1986   2468/22

Earl King, Stevie Ray Vaughan, and Dave Bartholomew, 1986   2464/37

AT LEFT:
Stevie Ray Vaughan, 1986   2460/25a

George Porter on drums with the Neville Brothers, 1986   2458/23

The Temptations: Otis Williams, Melvin Franklin, Ron Tyson, Richard Street, Ollie Woodson, 1986   2465/31

Olympia Jr. Brass Band: Revert Andrews (trombone), Abraham Cosse (tuba), Stafford Agee (trombone), Wendell ? (saxophone), Derek Shezbie (trumpet), Kenneth Terry (trumpet), Cytanio Hingle (bass drum), Glenn Andrews (trumpet), Frank ? (tap dance), 1986   2468/3

Food, 1987   2564/17

Saxons Superstars, 1987   2564/11

Fair Grounds map, 1987   2567/3

The Zion Harmonizers: Nolan Washington, Alvin Thomas, Howard Bowie, Joe Warrick, Sherman Washington (leader), and Willie Williams, 1987   2566/3

The Treme Sports Social and Pleasure Club parade: Landry ("Fat Man") Grandison and Charles Taylor, 1987   2564/29

WWOZ interview with Ramsey McLean and Charles Neville by Jason Patterson, 1987   2572/15

Reggie Houston (sax), Charmaine Neville (vocals), Charles Neville (sax), Ramsey McLean (bass), 1987   2571/9a

Mike Stark (staff) with Pete Seeger, 1987   2573/8

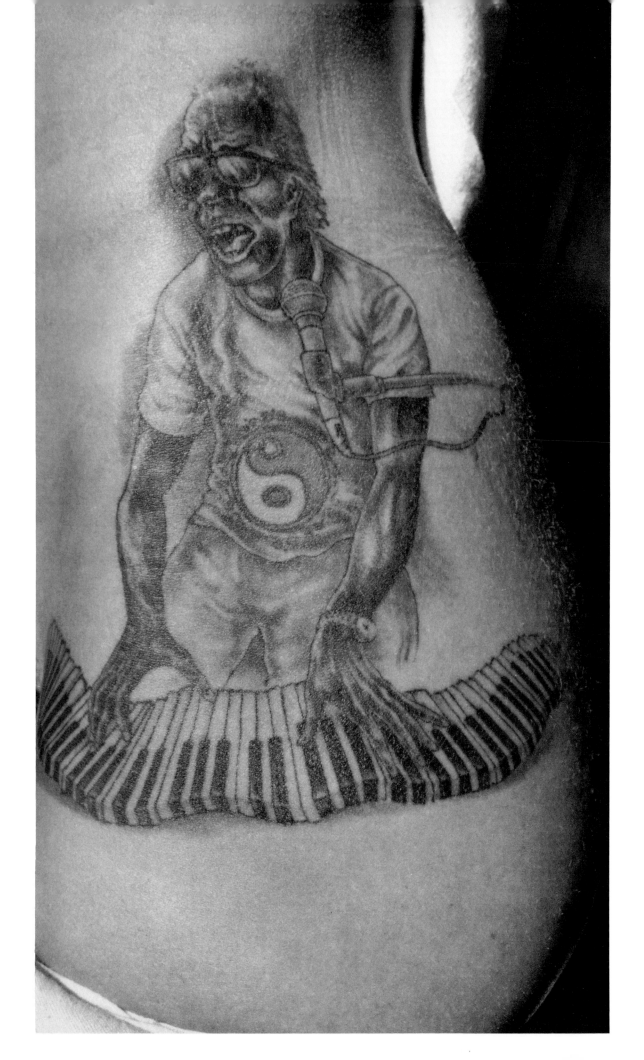

Pharoah Sanders, 1987   2573/6

Harry Connick, Jr., 1987   2571/15a

AT LEFT:
Professor Longhair tattoo (on the hip of Marjorie
Knight, staff), 1987   2567/36

Robert Cray, 1987   2570/20

The Four Tops: Abdul ("Duke") Fakir, Renaldo ("Obie") Benson, Laurence Payton, and Levi Stubbs, 1987   2564/9

Beausoleil: Michael Doucet (fiddle), Pat Breaux (accordion), 1987   2562/25

John Rankin and mother, Betty ("Big Mama") Rankin, 1987   2570/13

Dr. John and Barbara ("B. B.") Becker, his road manager,
1987   2573/35

Ron Kottemann, Roman Candy man, 1987   2571/4a

Treme Sports with Stanley Jackson and Cornelius Fizer (grand marshalls) followed by the Second Line Jammers, with the Chosen Few Brass Band (Elliot "Stackman" Callier, sax; Darryl Adams, trombone; and Eddie Paris, trombone), 1987 2572/2

Chosen Few Brass Band rhythm section: Kenneth Austin (snare drum), Michael Jones (bass drum), Benny Jones (snare drum), 1987 2572/11

Parade: Doc Paulin (trumpet), Ricky Paulin (drum), 1987 2569/6

Bad weather, 1988   2662/14a

Webo O'Neill makes a special announce-
ment, 1988   2672/30

Los Lobos: Cesar Rojas and David Hidalgo,
1988   2662/7

Judge Reinhold visits Los Lobos backstage, 1988   2667/13a

Los Lobos: Cesar Rojas, David Hidalgo, and Steve Berlin, 1988   2673/4

Katie Webster, 1988   2694/15a

David Hidalgo, Los Lobos, 1988   2673/20

Jimmy Ballero, George Porter, and Amasa Miller with the Pfister Sisters (Susy Malone, Holly Bendtsen, and Yvette Volker), 1988   2665/32a

Amasa Miller (keyboard), George Porter (bass), and Jimmy Ballero (guitar) with the Pfister Sisters, 1988   2665/12a

Taj Mahal with George Porter on bass, 1988   2693/17

Little Feat: Paul Barrere (guitar), Bill Payne (keyboard), Craig Fuller (guitar), Kenny Gradney (bass), Fred Tackett (guitar), Richie Hayward (drums), 1988   2662/30

Little Feat on Riverboat: Fred Tackett (guitar), Kenny Gradney (bass), Bill Payne (keyboard), Craig Fuller (guitar), Paul Barrere (guitar), 1988   2663/7a

Bonnie Raitt with Little Feat (on boat), 1988   2678/33

Crowd, 1988   2661/23

James Brown, 1988   2689/8

Group masking at the fair, 1988   2686/7

Casa Samba, 1988   2685/26a

167

Jim Jenkins, blacksmith, 1988   2698/23a

Music Heritage Tent: Allison Miner presents Marce Lacatoure, Inez Catalan, and Lula Landry for Cajun songs and stories, 1988   2693/2

Hank Ballard sings "Annie Had a Baby" with stage manager Ed White's son, 1988   2661/32

Dr. John, 1988   2668/19

Irma Thomas, 1988   2680/11a

Potato Valdez, 1988 2689/16

Li'l Queenie (Leigh Harris) and Ramsey McLean (bass), 1988 2686/37

Jessie Hill, 1988 2681/10a

Allen Toussaint playing guitar/keyboard, 1988   2691/17

The Valley of Silent Men Social & Pleasure Club parade with the Re-Birth Jazz Band: Kermit Ruffins (trumpet), John Gilbert (saxophone), Derek Shezbie (trumpet), 1988   2697/16

Miles Davis, Joseph ("Foley") McCreary, 1989   2852/19

Wynton Marsalis big band (in the River Tent): Herlin Riley (drums), Lucien Barbarin (trombone), Michael White (clarinet), Todd Williams (tenor sax), Wes Anderson (alto saxophone), Teddy Riley (trumpet), Wynton Marsalis (trumpet), Danny Barker (banjo guitar), 1989   2849/13

172

John Hiatt, 1989   2833/34

John Lee Hooker, 1989   2870/16a

Evangeline: Rhonda Lohmeyer, Sharon Leger, Jan Polopolus, Leslie Smith-Doyle, 1989   2836/27

John Lee Hooker, 1989   2870/2a

Mason Ruffner, 1989   2857/3

Daniel Lanois, 1989   2856/19

Charles Neville and Harry Connick, Jr., 1989   2847/15

Wynton Marsalis poses with friend, 1989   2841/13

Beer "boat," 1989   2866/12

Beer trash, 1989   2867/15

Albertine Norwood with Creole African-
French cloth dolls, 1989   2838/32a

Irvin Perez, duck decoy booth, 1989
2848/35

Frank Vought, knife maker, 1989   2862/9

"Victory": silk painting demonstration, 1989   2862/2

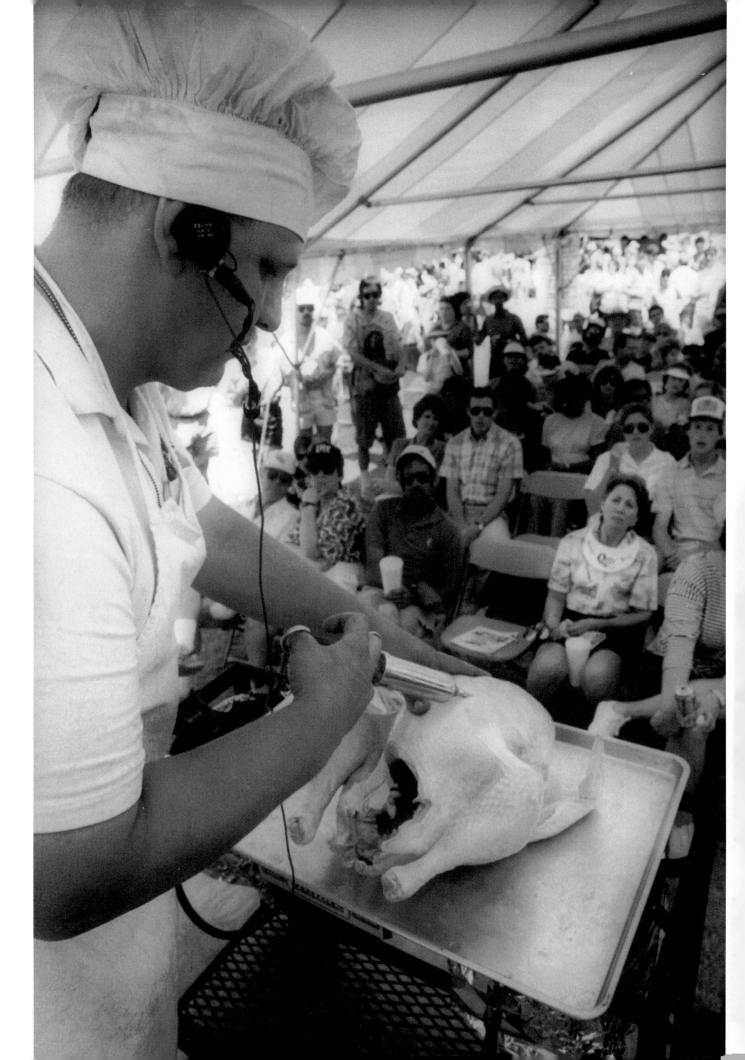

Boat building, 1989   2869/29a

AT LEFT:
Food demonstration: G. R. McIlhennie prepares deep-fried turkey with a shot of Tabasco sauce, 1989   2861/8a

Congo Square, 1989   2869/24a

Allison Miner presents Allen Toussaint at the Music Heritage Tent, 1989   2861/23a

Alton ("Rockin' Dopsie") Rubin, "King of Zydeco," Larry Jolvet (bass), Paul ("Buck") Senegal (guitar), and David Rubin, "Master of the Rhythm" (frattoir), 1989   2859/24

Festival History Photo Booth in Heritage Village, 1989   2837/33a

Earl King visits Michael P. Smith's photo
booth, 1989   2859/5

Crafts, 1989   2837/14a

Craft Village, 1989   2867/24

The Second-Line Jammers Social & Pleasure Club parade: Clara Joseph, Bridgett Degrui, and group, 1989   2870/32a

The Subdudes: Steve Amadee (percussion), John Magnie (accordion), Tommy Malone (guitar), and Johnny Allen (bass), 1989   2863/19

Leo Nocentelli and George Porter, 1989   2839/30a

The Radiators: David Malone (guitar), Reggie Scanlan, Eddie Volker (keyboard and vocals), Camille Baudoin (percussion), Frank Bua (drums), 1989   2872/22

Sun Ra, 1989   2864/28

Sun Ra and friend, 1989   2864/11

Michael Ray (lead trumpet) with Sun Ra,
1989   2864/5

The Turtle Shell Band from Belize, 1989   2840/31a

African stilt dancers, 1989   2840/5a

Jam on stage 1: Steve Allen (saxophone), Jimmy Buffet (guitar), Rita Coolidge, Ed Bradley, Priscilla Coolidge, New Orleans Mayor Sidney Barthelemy, 1989   2845/31a

Priscilla Coolidge, Charmaine Neville, and Rita Coolidge, 1989   2842/22

"Tent city" at the stage 4 outfield, 1989   2862/17

Tent city, 1989   2862/18

Melody Clouds, 1989   2862/37

Tent city, 1989   2862/21

Signpost, 1990   2932/32

Al Johnson, 1990   2940/13

Eddie Bo, 1990   2934/27a

Champion Jack Dupree, 1990   2939/14

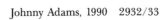

Johnny Adams, 1990   2932/33

Marva Wright, 1990   2940/21

"Coco" Brown (vocals) with Charles Neville in Mars Jazz Tent, 1990   2948/8

Tommy Ridgley and the Untouchables, 1990   2948/31

Joe ("Mr. Google Eyes") August, 1990
2951/6

Folk Arts Village: O. L. Samuels, wood-carver, 1990   2936/32a

Zachary Richard, 1990   2935/37

Terrance Simien, 1990   2941/30

Boozoo Chavis, 1990   2932/5a

Backstage business: producer of the Telluride Jazz Festival pitches to Boz Scaggs, 1990   2944/19a

Celia Cruz, 1990   2941/25

Congo Square, 1990   2933/15

Howard ("Smilie") Ricks (Big Chief, Wild Comanche Hunters), Donald Harrison, Sr. (Big Chief, Guardians of the Flame), with the Kabuka Dancers, 1990   2934/34

Mahlathini and the Mahatolla Queens, 1990 2937/24a

The Mahatolla Queens of South Africa, 1990   2937/9a

Toots and the Maytals, 1990   2931/33

Flaco Jimenez, 1990   2935/11

Jeanette Kimbell, 1990   2932/10a

Bo Diddley presents Troy Michael Andrews on trombone, 1990 2953/20

Bo Diddley (Elias Bates McDaniel), 1990 2953/2

Ernest ("Doc") Paulin (trumpet), Ricky Paulin (drum), with the Doc Paulin Brass Band, 1990 2933/33

Tipitina's/Sweet Molasses (arts on the infield), 1990 2933/17

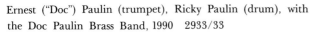

Linda Ronstadt and Aaron Neville,
1990 2932/28a

The Neville Brothers, 1990   2946/23

Afterword

Traditional Culture and Recreation:
Not to Kill Time, but to Enrich Time

Amusement is a relatively mindless form of entertainment. People amuse themselves by playing passive and inane games of chance like slot machines. One can be amused by purchasing a thrill — such as one might find in an amusement park. Amusement in general is a self-indulgent activity, devoid of primary human interaction and learning potential. It is a subcategory of entertainment; its function is to kill time.

Entertainment should be differentiated from amusement as requiring active use of the intellect and other sensory skills. It involves direct or indirect interaction with other human beings and has a view to the future. Reading, traditional games of skill such as chess or bridge, sophisticated electronic games (which require learning skills applicable to other activities), or observing creative human performance might be considered entertainment. Entertainment, however, is a relatively limited and passive form of leisure.

Recreation (re-creation), by contrast, should be considered the most comprehensive form of physical and spiritual sustenance. Recreation goes beyond amusement and entertainment in that it actively utilizes physical, intellectual, and spiritual elements of being. It involves the whole self — body, mind, and soul — and entails primary community interaction and involvement. Recreation re-affirms identity, builds character, and contributes to the expansion of knowledge, or the improvement of life; it is not self-oriented. It is life affirming, usually involves family participation, and generally works toward bringing people together to celebrate their heritage and culture — their own unique contributions to life. Participation in traditional cultural activities can be considered recreation — active involvement in religious celebration, creative sports, dance, music, etc. Exercising one's creative talents is recreation. Recreation involves active participation in and appreciation of life.

The New Orleans Jazz & Heritage Festival provides a setting for cultural recreation of the best sort. From the first presentation of this event in 1970 participants were filled with song, dance, and hearty food, and surrounded by traditional family values and atmosphere. Performers were happily involved as well because

199

they appreciated the inclusive quality of the event. For the performers it was like playing for a traditional family picnic — where the audience and performers were all part of the same community sharing equally in the celebration of life. The Jazz & Heritage Festival has achieved such success because it celebrates and builds upon the great port city's unique history of cross-fertilization and refinement of world musics and cultures.

It is now widely known that the regional cultural heritages presented each year at the Jazz Fest are alive and can be found here at all times of the year. Increasingly, film crews from all parts of the globe come here all year long hoping to document our legendary regional culture in authentic context. This publicity is rebounding to bring tourists to New Orleans at all times of the year. New Orleans, especially for African-Americans, is rapidly becoming a Mecca for people seeking significant living examples of cultural diversity and ethnic heritage in America.

In considering the tremendous financial rewards and other benefits the festival has brought to New Orleans we are constrained to reappraise the value of our unique heritage. Some of this heritage — the Mardi Gras Indians, for example, an African cultural heritage submerged in the inner city for more than a century — was recognized by the Jazz & Heritage Festival and presented to outside audiences for the first time in 1970. The Mardi Gras Indians are now considered a national treasure. Among other things these groups preserve the drumming traditions and culture, brought to New Orleans from Africa, which were fundamental to the development of jazz.

The Jazz Fest has also brought much needed recognition to the annual parades of the Second Line clubs in New Orleans, an African-American cultural tradition also influential in the birth of jazz in New Orleans. The present-day activities of these clubs are essential to the continuation of jazz as a living heritage in the city.

The success and prosperity of the Jazz Fest suggests that the City of New Orleans might be advised to recognize and encourage the development of its culture and music all year long . . . perhaps build upon the experience of the festival to create a City Park of Music and Cultural Heritage. Such a park, highlighting and promoting existing resources in the city, could serve as a sanctuary and strategic access center for our cultural heritage resources. It would be easy and inexpensive to establish, relevant to the life and economy of the city, and supportive of our greatest and most endangered resources. The Jazz Fest, in fact, is a perfect model for such a park, and Armstrong Park would be the ideal location.

With cultural heritage now being a primary tourist attraction in New Orleans, and a vast underdeveloped economic resource, Armstrong Park could serve as a center to preserve, encourage, and coordinate the development of our rich traditions, performance arts, cuisine arts, and music. It is clear now that these things are among our city's greatest assets, and certainly constitute the most profound basis for social and economic revitalization that is much needed in the modern city.

Index

Flaco Jimenez, 1990   2935/21